VOL. 5

HAL•LEONARD MANDOLIN PLAY-ALONG

Gypsy Swing

T0083881

Mandolin by Mike Cramer

ISBN 978-1-4584-1394-9

HAL•LEONARD® CORPORATION

7777 W. BLUEMOUND RD. P.O. BOX 13819 MILWAUKEE, WI 53213

In Australia Contact:
Hal Leonard Australia Pty. Ltd.
4 Lentara Court
Cheltenham, Victoria, 3192 Australia
Email: ausadmin@halleonard.com.au

For all works contained herein:
Unauthorized copying, arranging, adapting, recording, Internet posting, public performance, or other distribution
of the printed or recorded music in this publication is an infringement of copyright.
Infringers are liable under the law.

Visit Hal Leonard Online at
www.halleonard.com

TRACK 1

After You've Gone

from ONE MO' TIME
Words by Henry Creamer
Music by Turner Layton

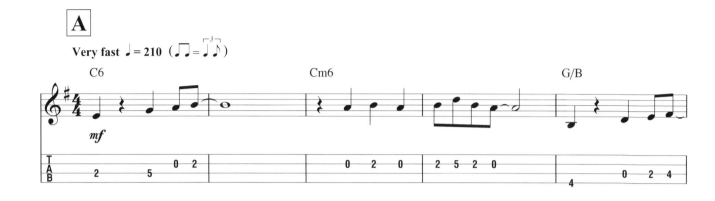

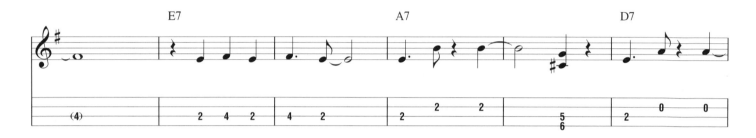

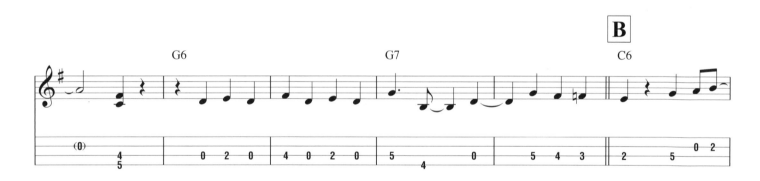

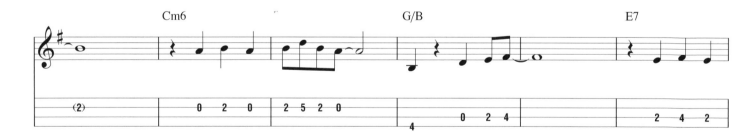

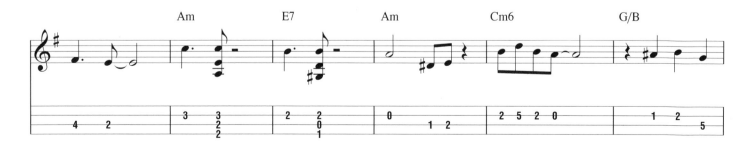

Copyright © 2015 by HAL LEONARD CORPORATION
International Copyright Secured   All Rights Reserved

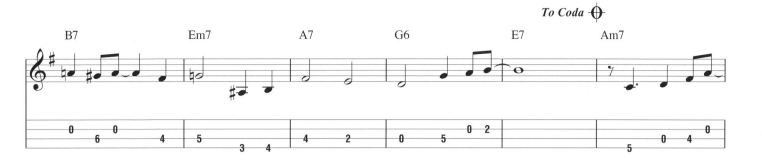

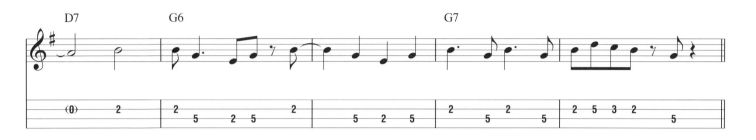

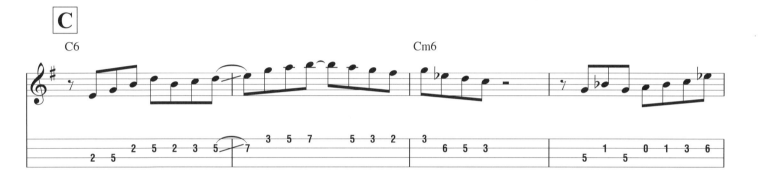

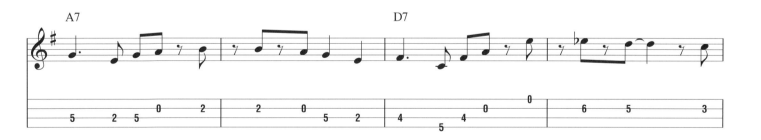

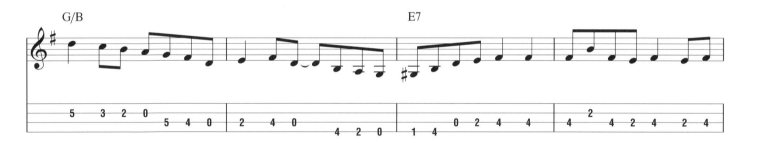

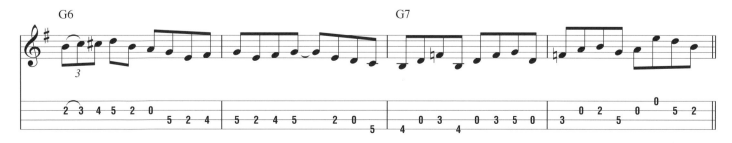

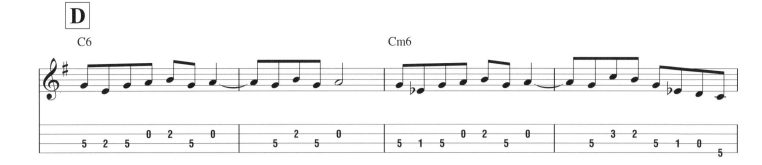

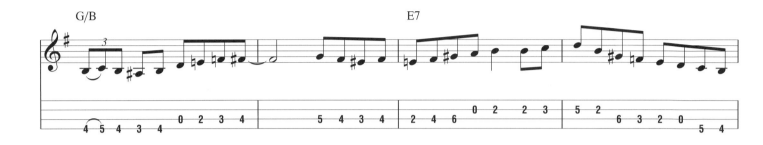

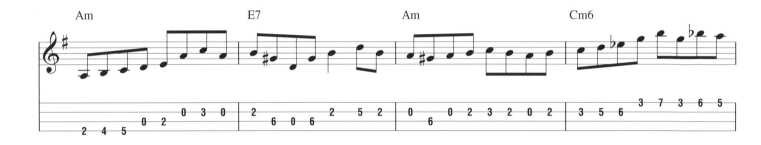

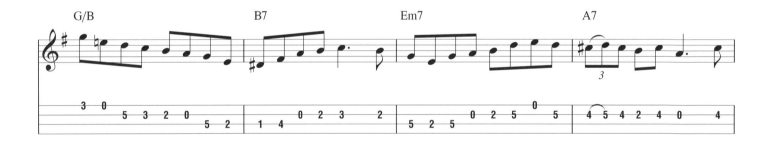

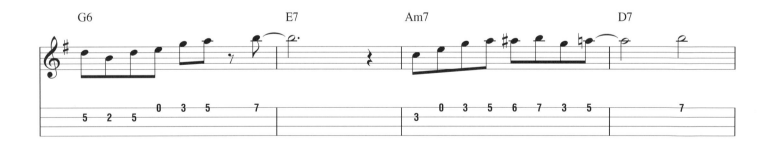

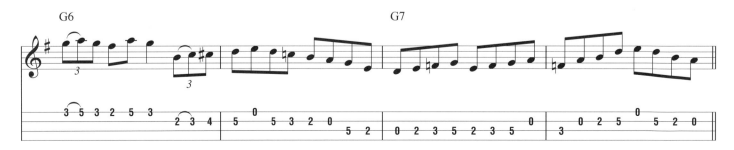

E

F

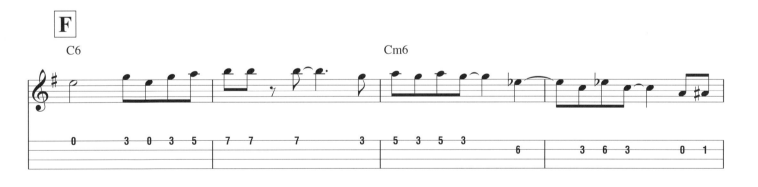

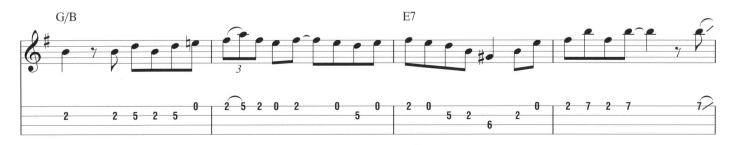

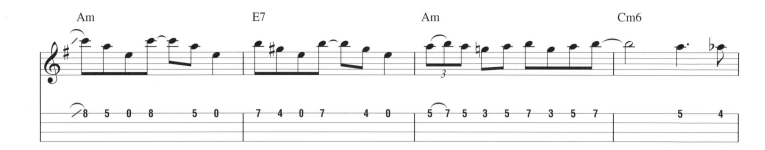

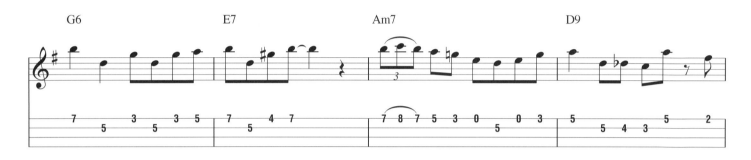

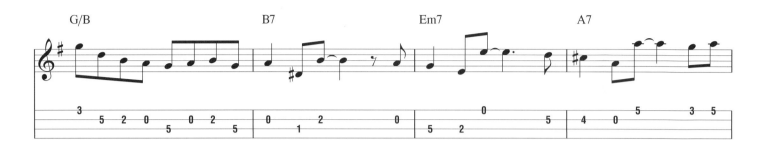

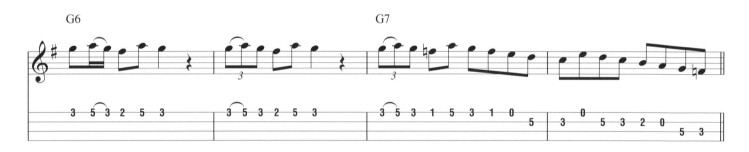

G

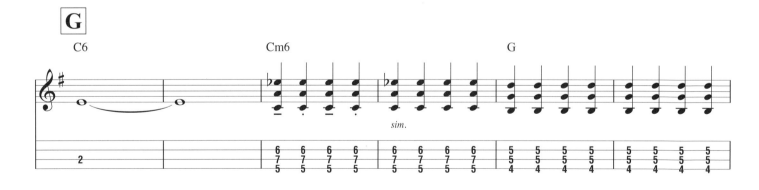

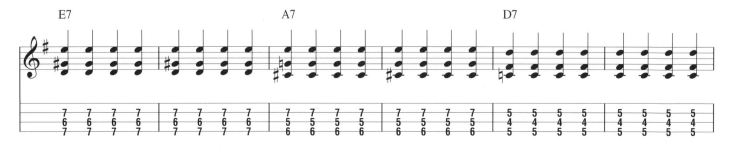

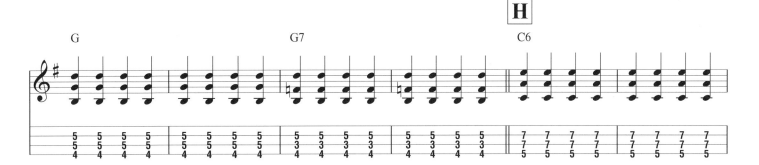

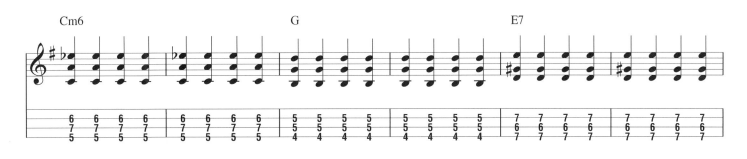

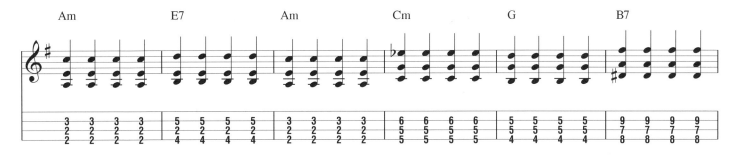

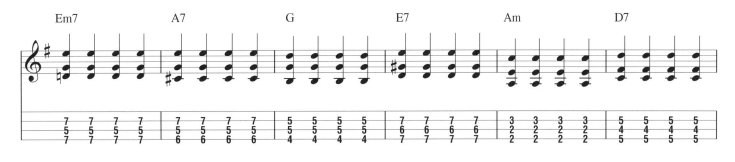

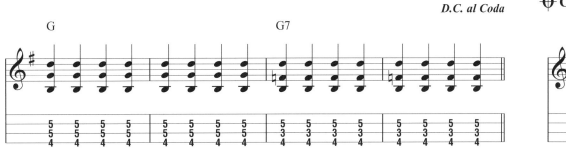

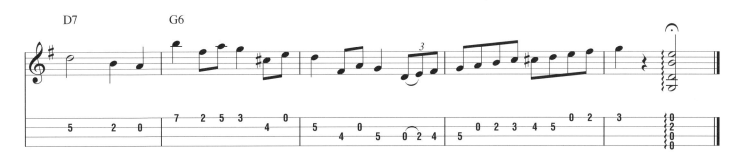

Avalon

Words by Al Jolson and B.G. DeSylva
Music by Vincent Rose

TRACK 3

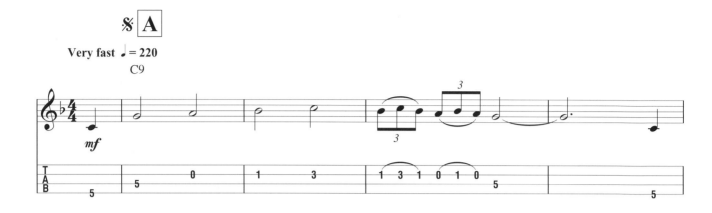

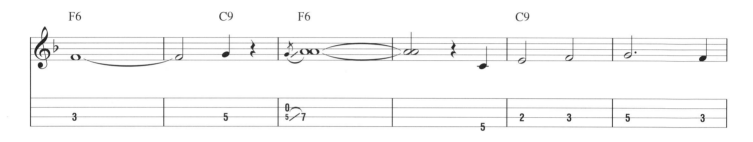

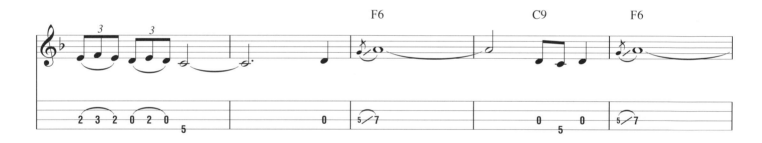

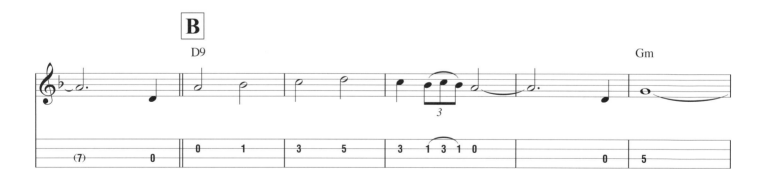

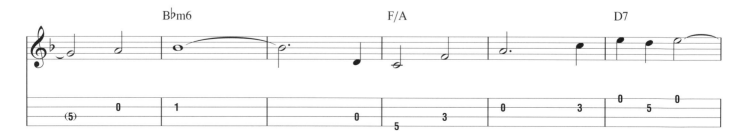

8

Copyright © 2015 by HAL LEONARD CORPORATION
International Copyright Secured   All Rights Reserved

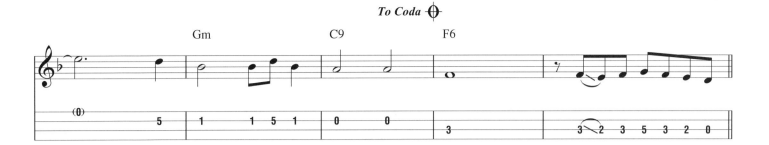

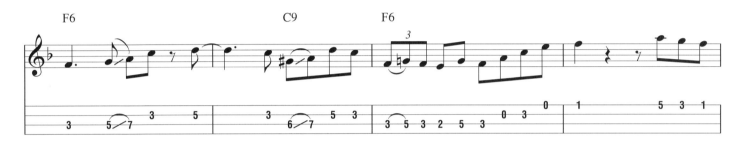

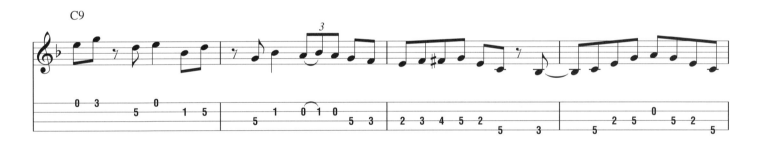

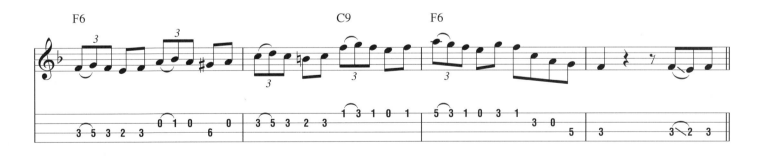

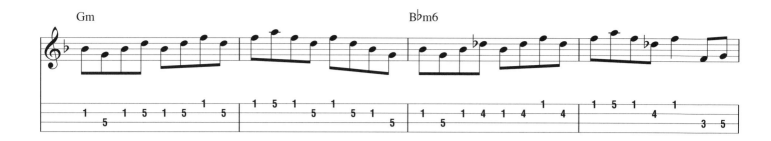

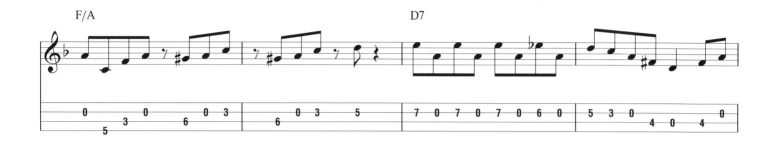

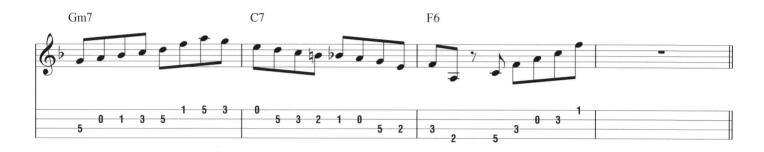

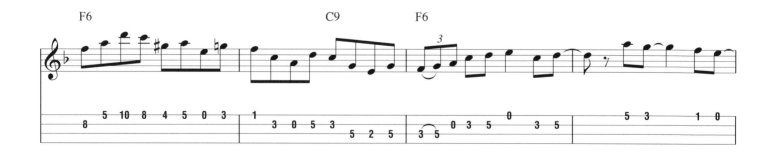

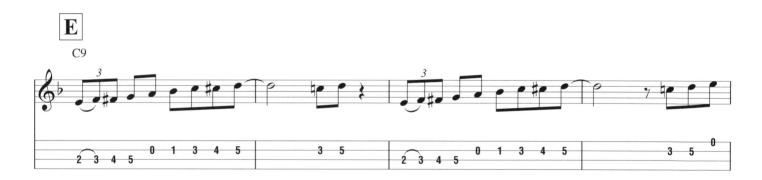

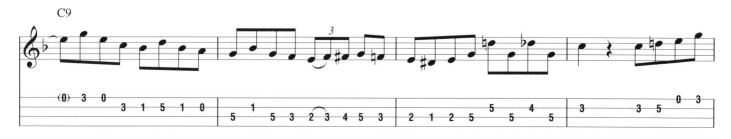

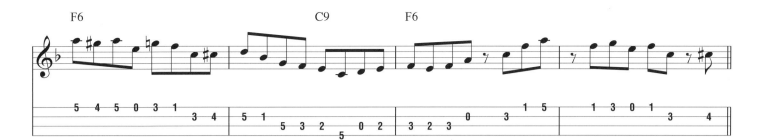

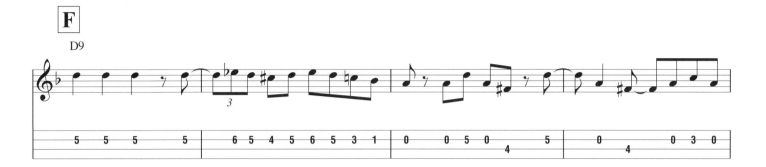

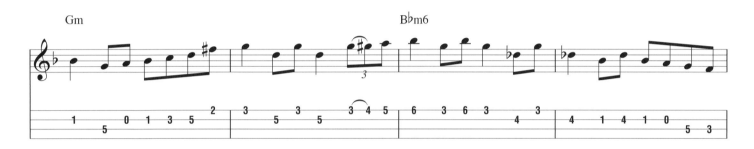

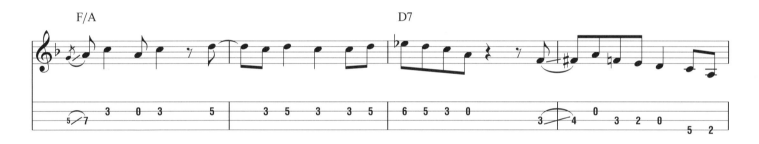

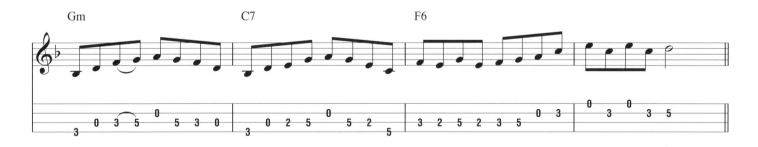

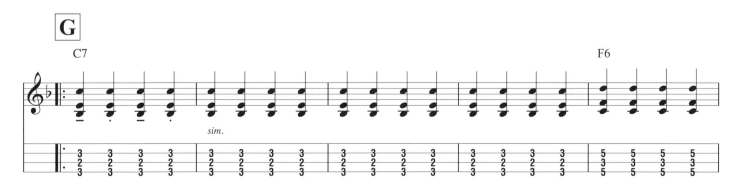

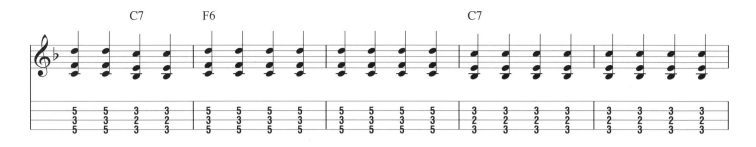

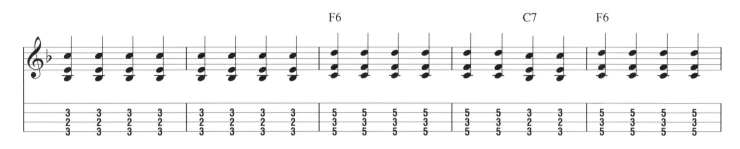

H

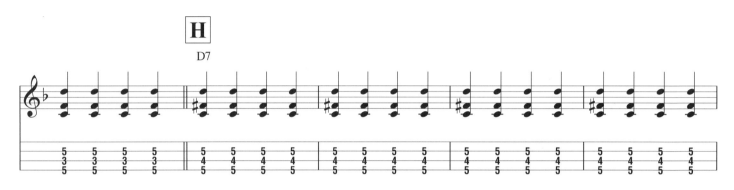

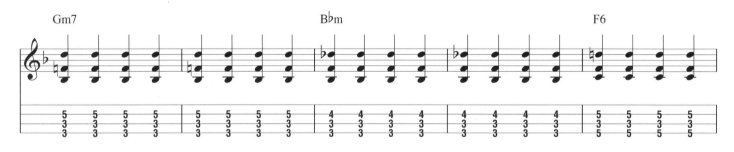

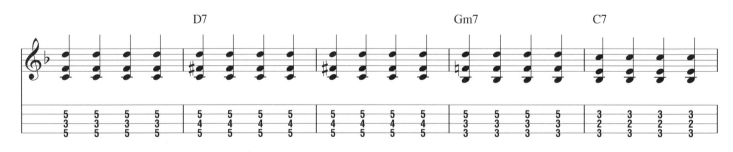

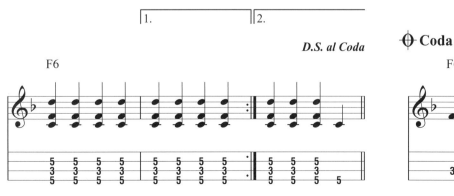

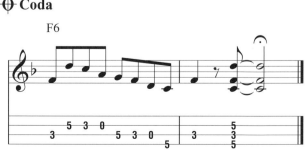

China Boy

Words and Music by Dick Winfree and Phil Boutelje

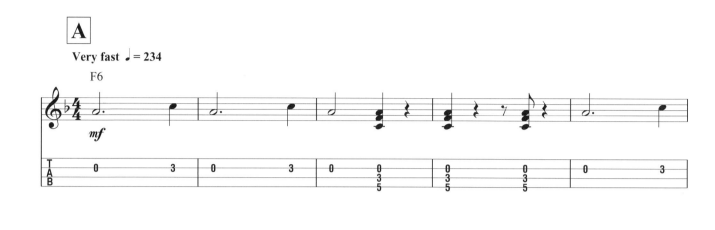

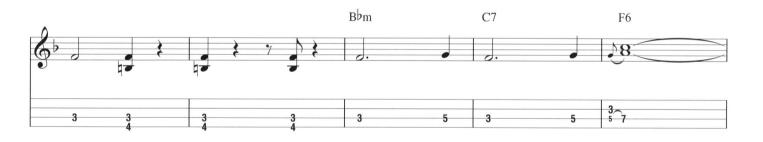

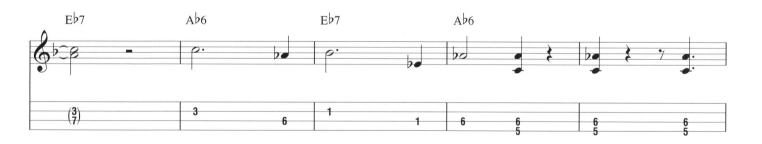

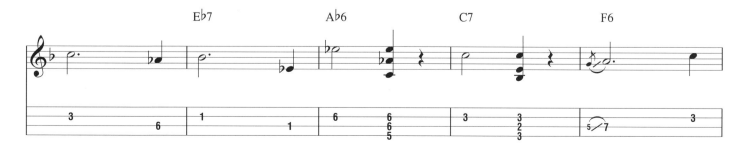

Copyright © 2015 by HAL LEONARD CORPORATION
International Copyright Secured   All Rights Reserved

B

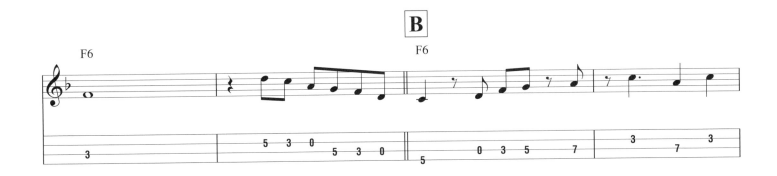

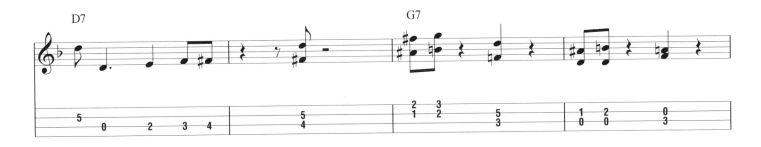

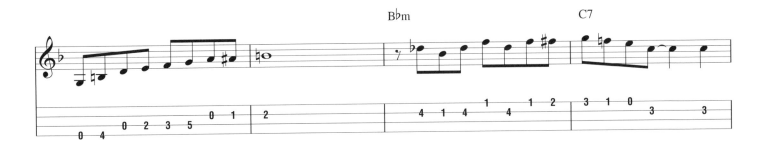

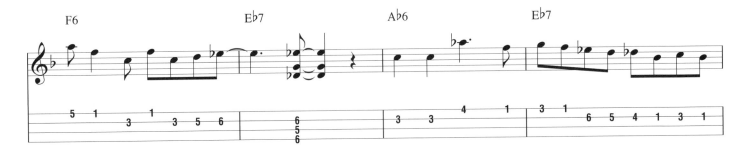

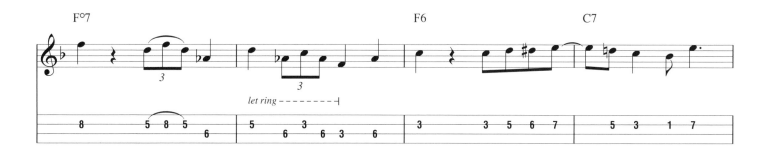

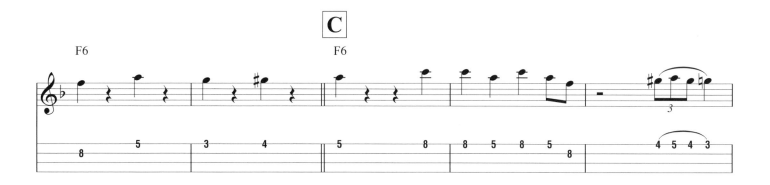

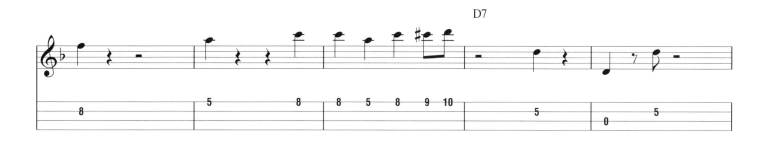

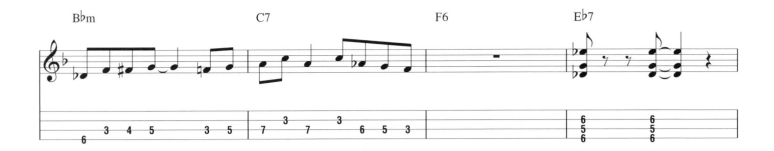

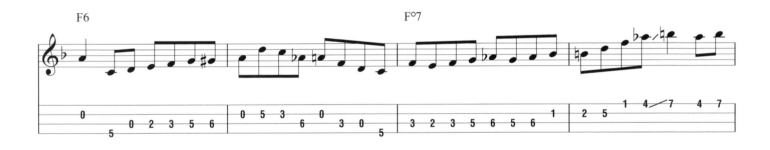

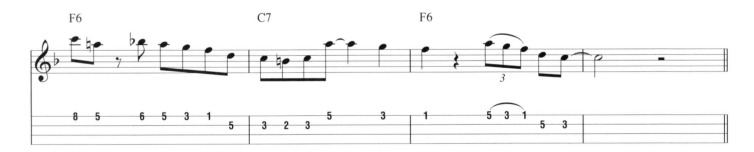

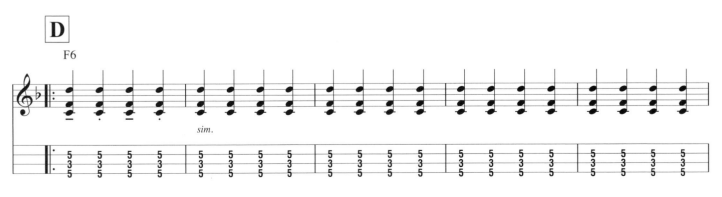

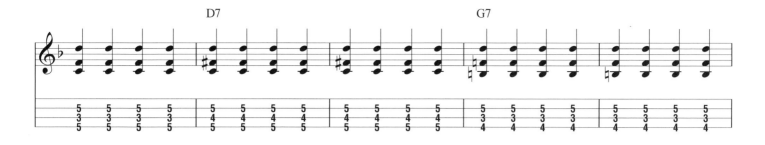

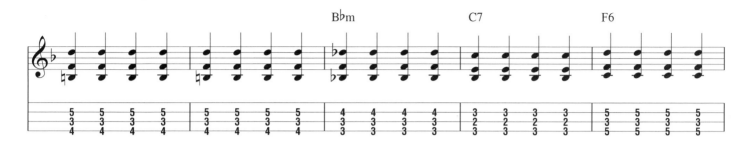

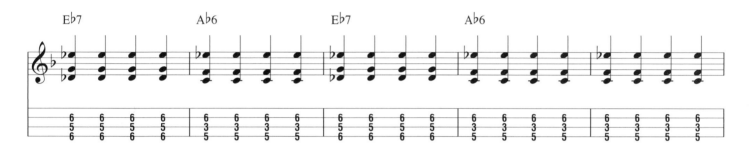

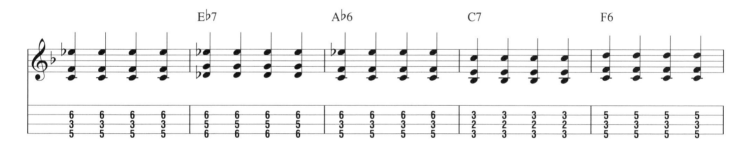

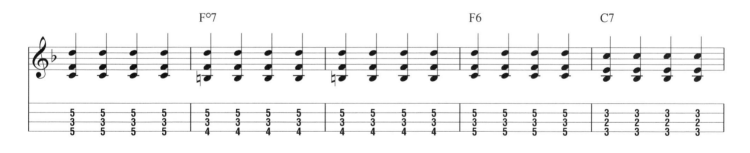

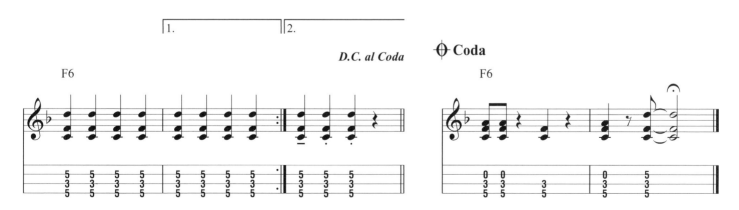

Dark Eyes

Russian Cabaret Song

TRACK 7

A

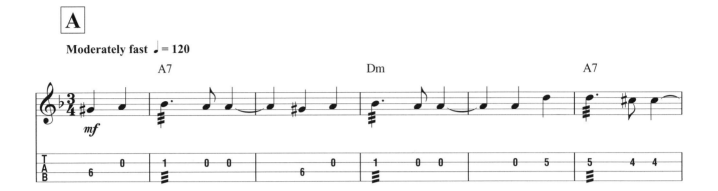

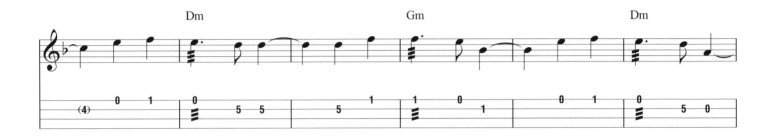

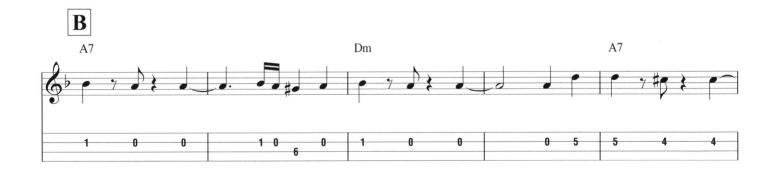

B

Copyright © 2015 by HAL LEONARD CORPORATION
International Copyright Secured   All Rights Reserved

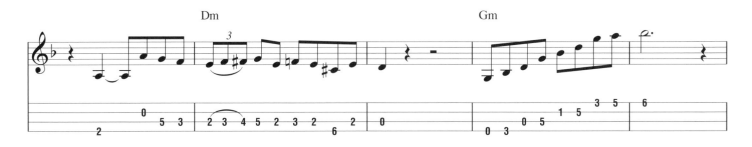

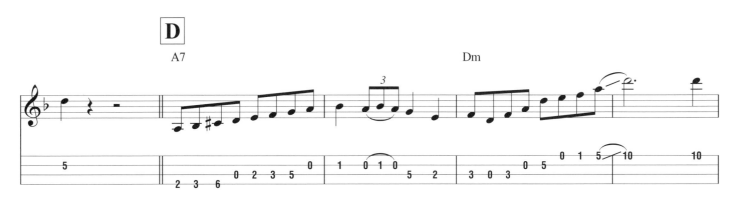

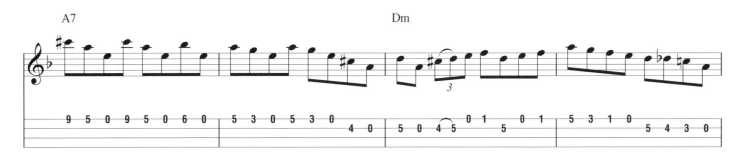

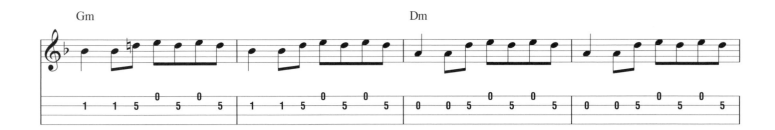

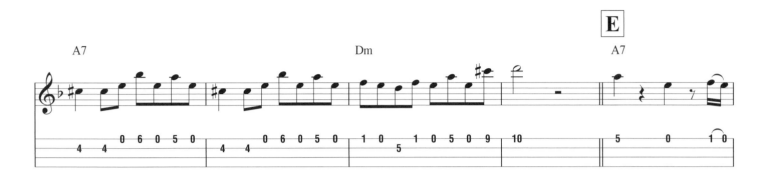

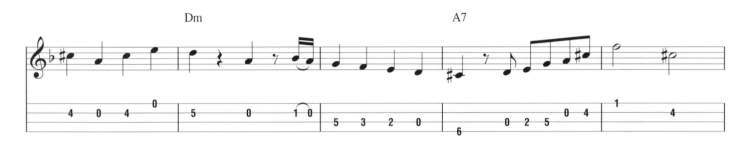

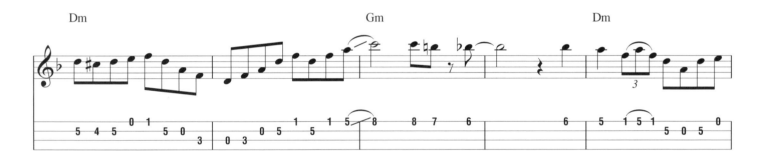

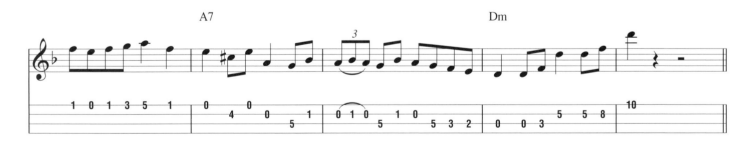

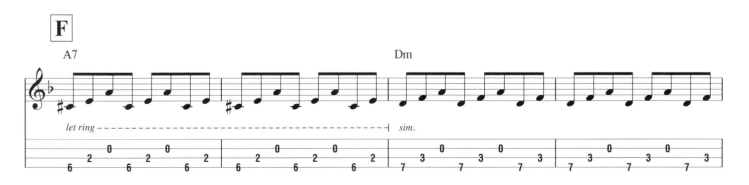

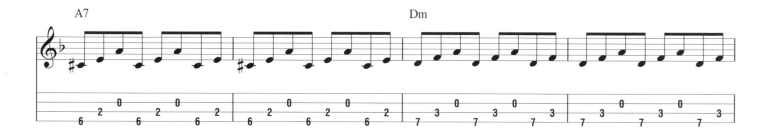

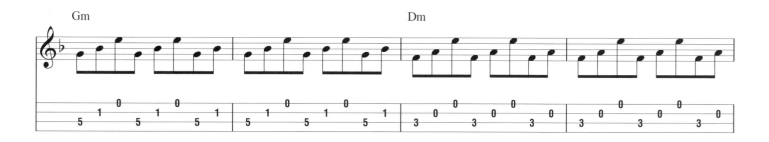

G

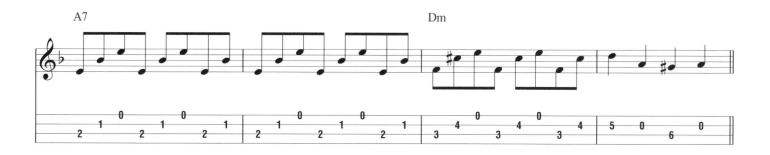

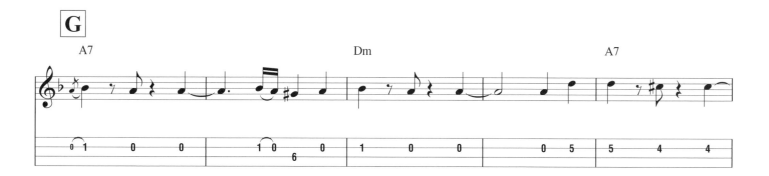

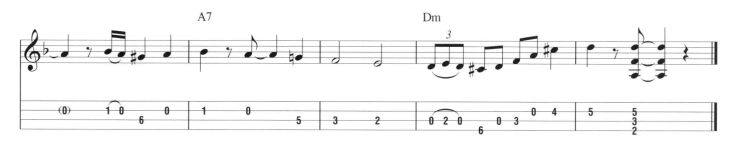

TRACK 9

Indiana
(Back Home Again in Indiana)

Words by Ballard MacDonald
Music by James F. Hanley

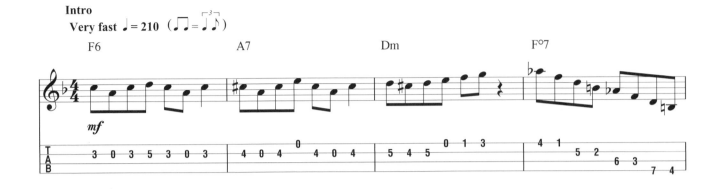

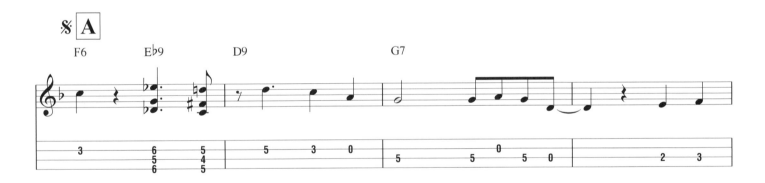

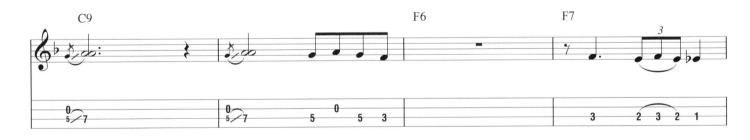

Copyright © 2015 by HAL LEONARD CORPORATION
International Copyright Secured   All Rights Reserved

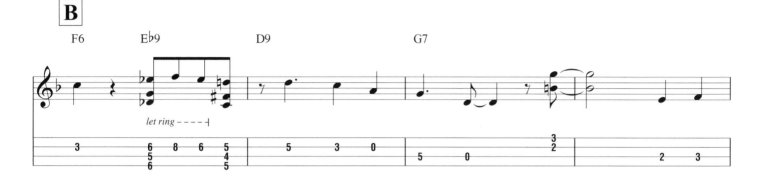

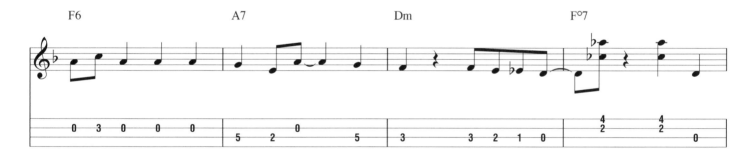

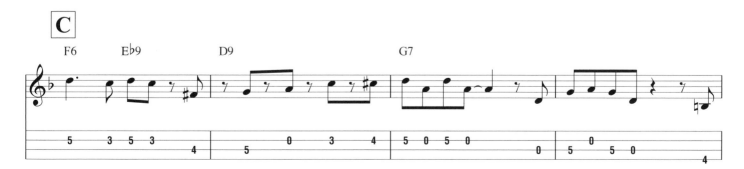

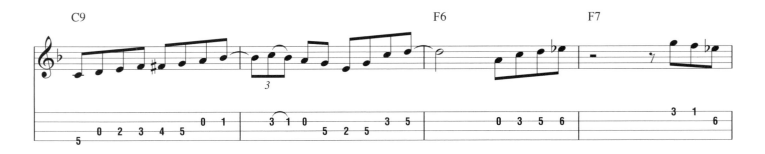

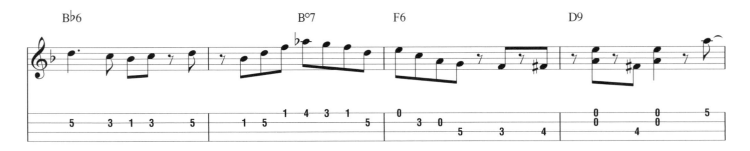

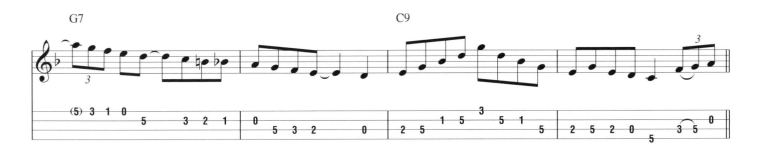

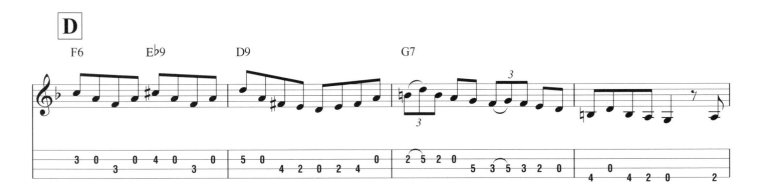

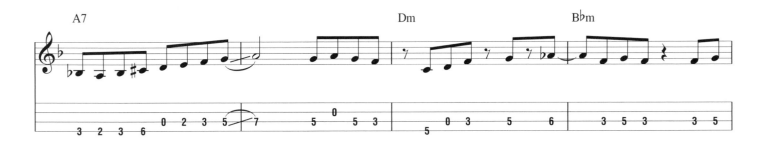

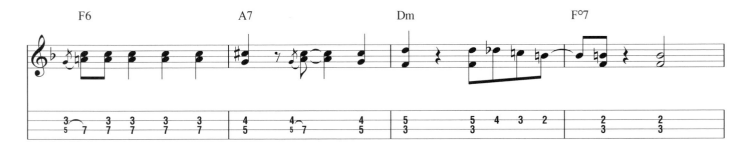

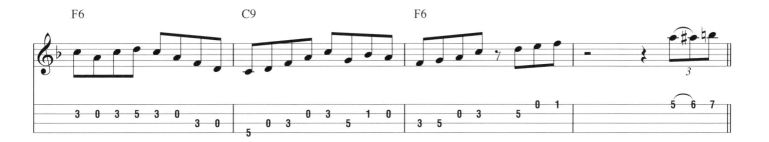

E

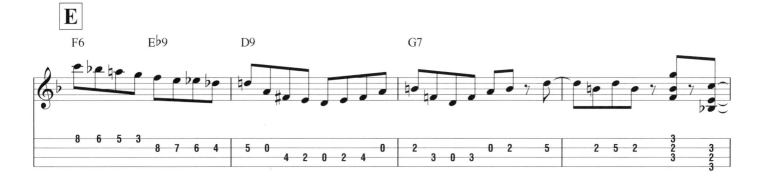

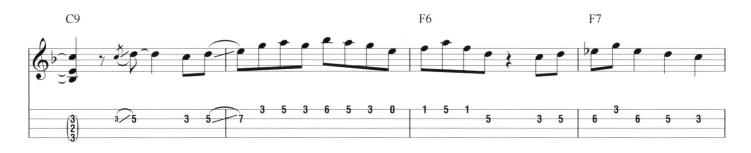

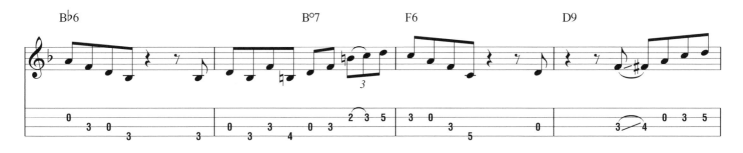

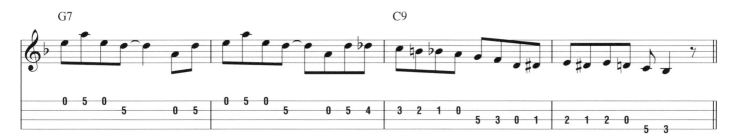

F

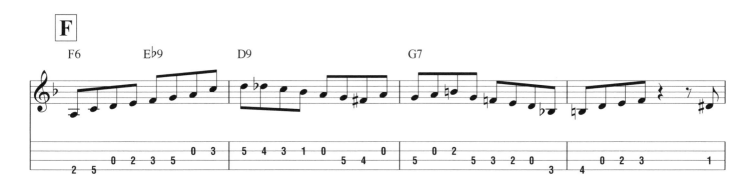

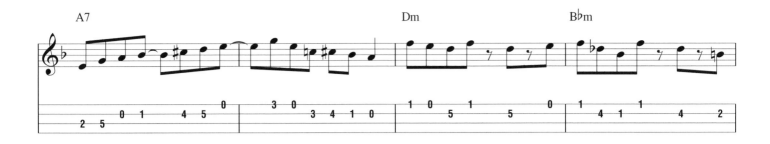

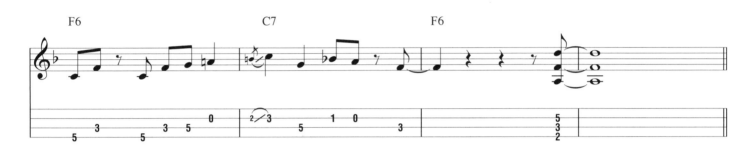

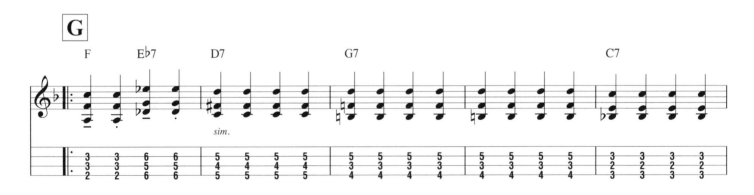

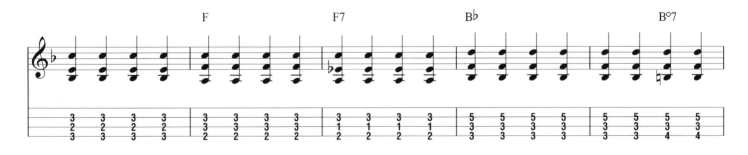

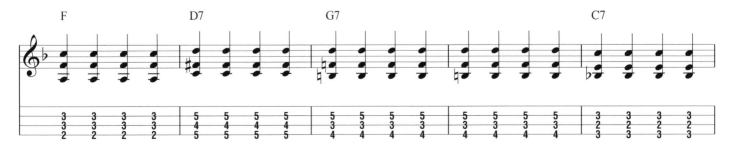

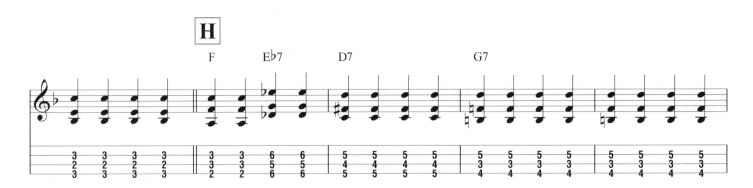

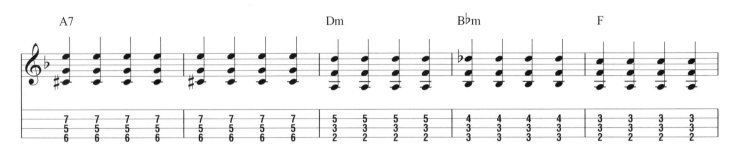

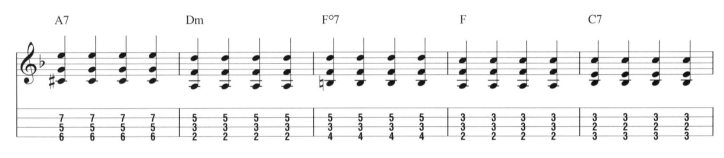

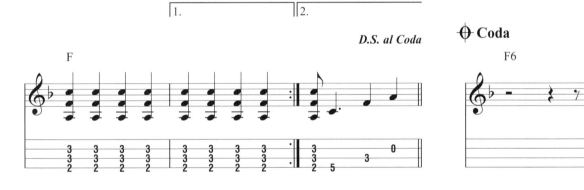

Outro

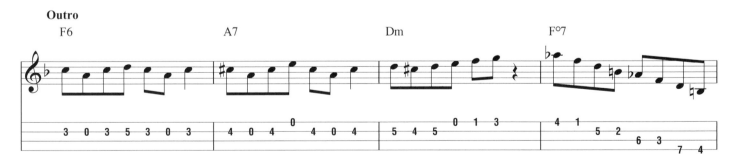

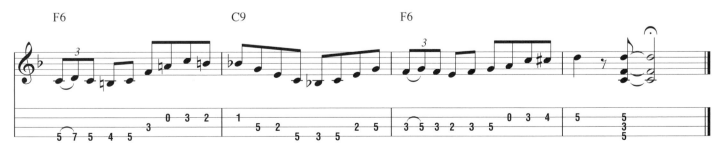

Limehouse Blues

from ZIEGFELD FOLLIES

Words by Douglas Furber
Music by Philip Braham

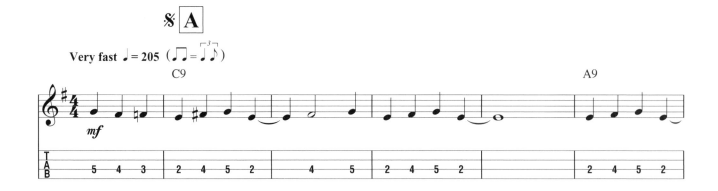

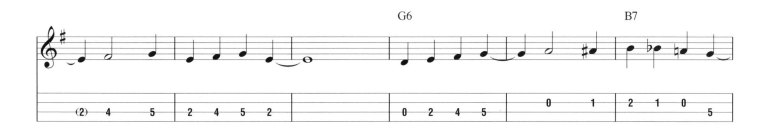

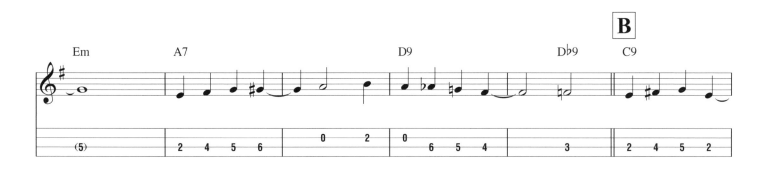

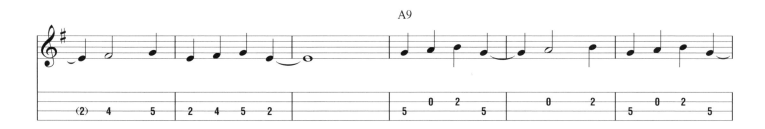

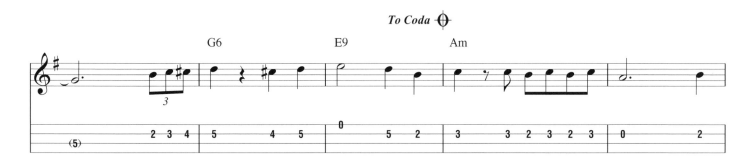

Copyright © 2015 by HAL LEONARD CORPORATION
International Copyright Secured   All Rights Reserved

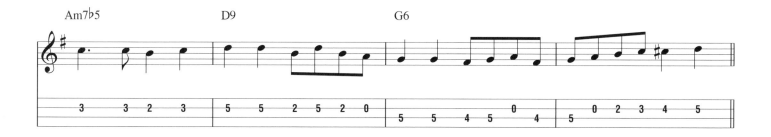

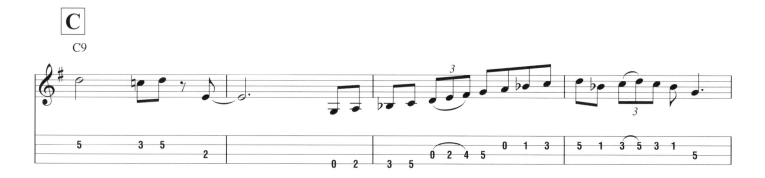

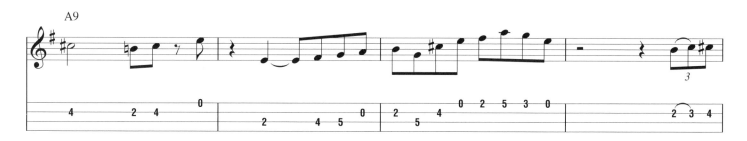

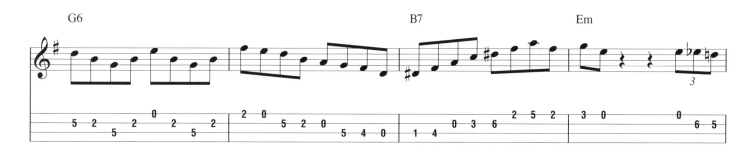

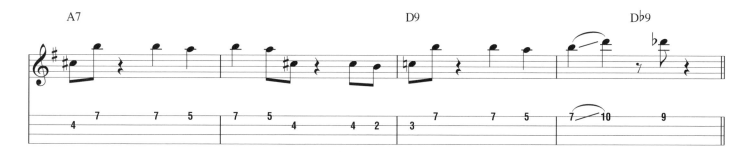

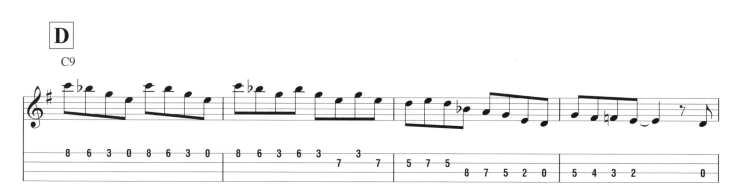

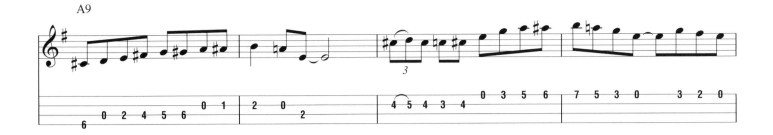

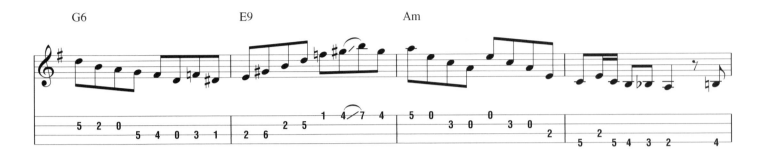

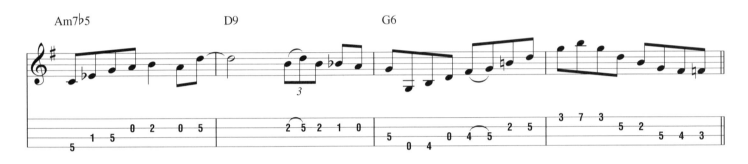

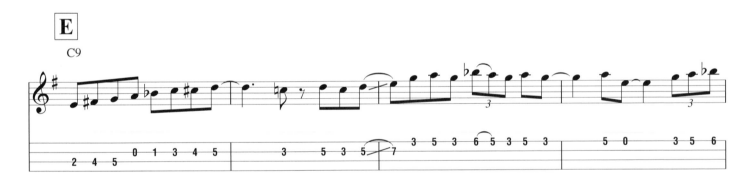

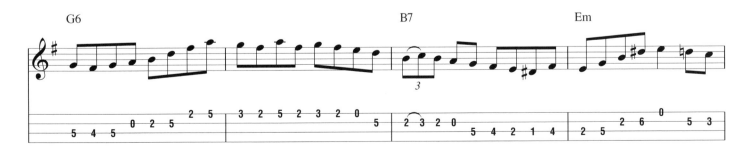

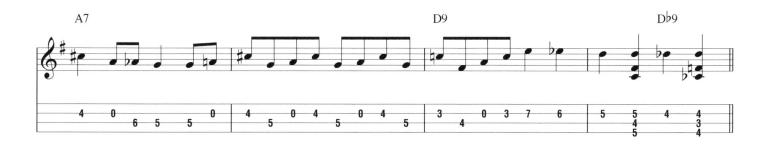

F

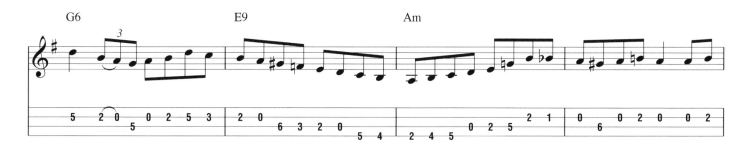

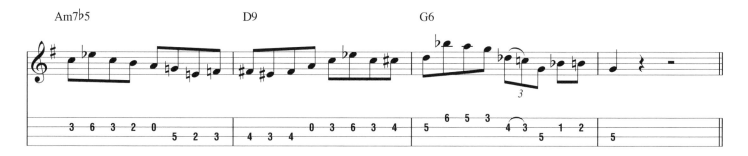

G

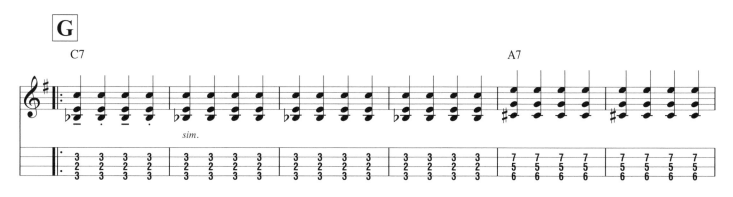

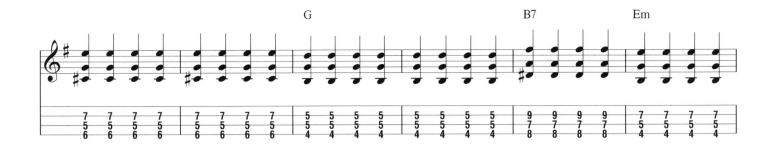

G   B7   Em

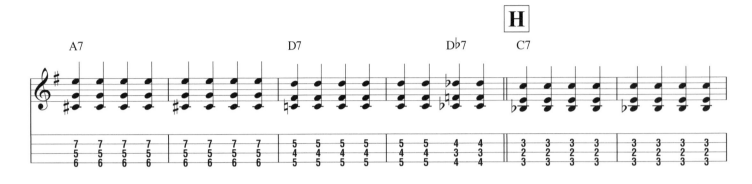

H

A7   D7   Db7   C7

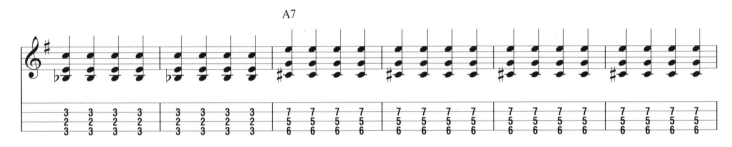

A7

G   E7   Am   Am7b5   D7

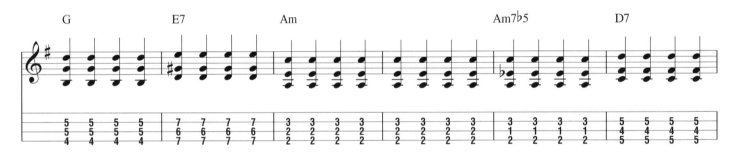

|1. |2.

D.S. al Coda   ⊕ **Coda**

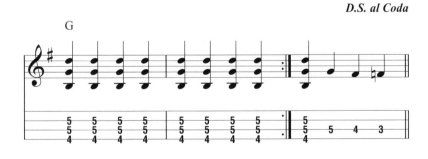

G   Am

Am7b5   D9   G6

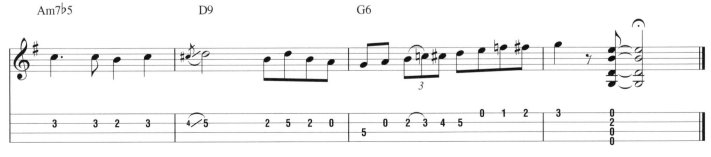

TRACK 15

Tiger Rag
(Hold That Tiger)

Words by Harry DeCosta
Music by Original Dixieland Jazz Band

A

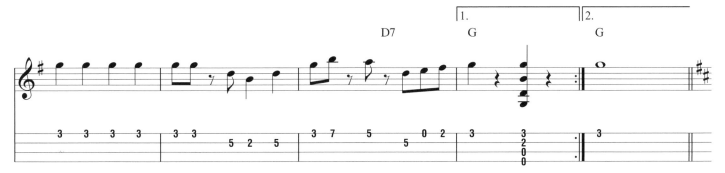

B

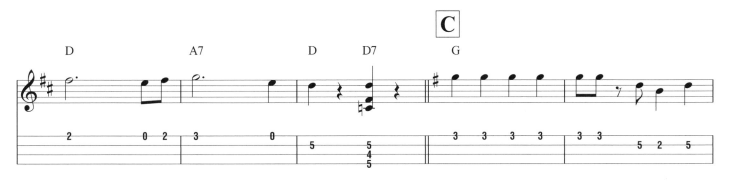

C

Copyright © 2015 by HAL LEONARD CORPORATION
International Copyright Secured   All Rights Reserved

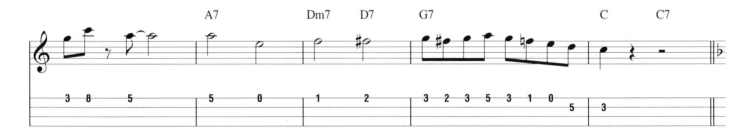

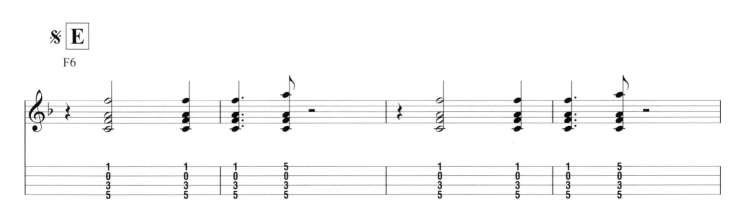

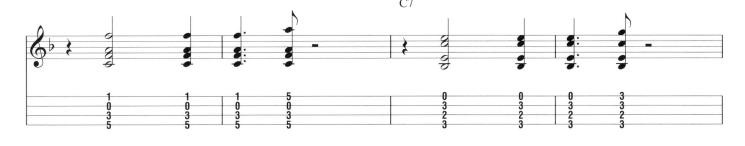

C7

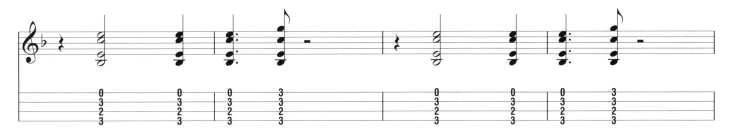

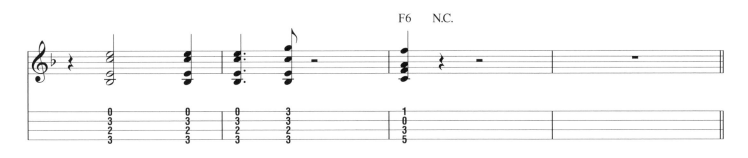

F6   N.C.

F

F6

Bb

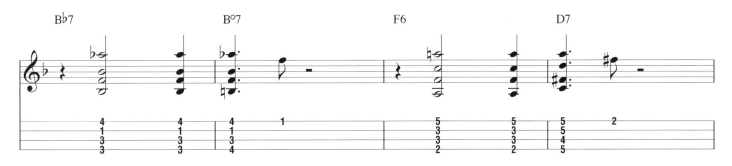

Bb7   B°7   F6   D7

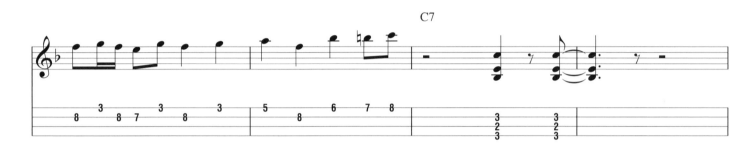

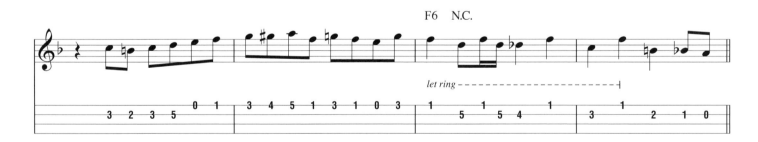

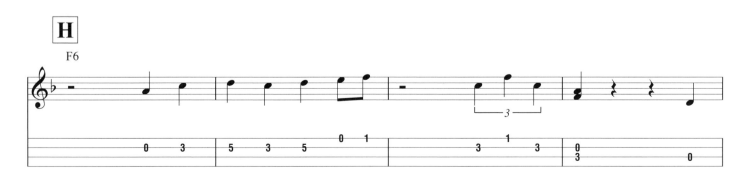

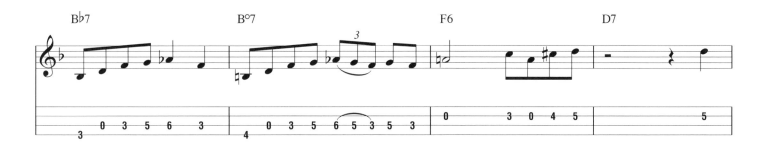

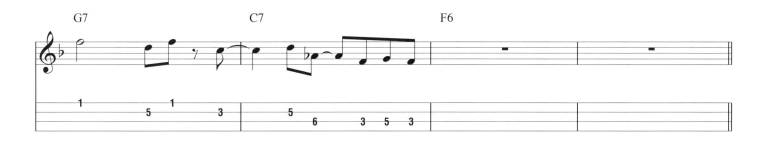

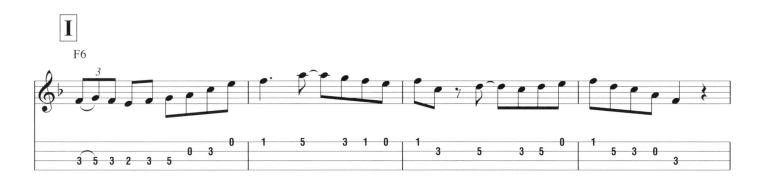

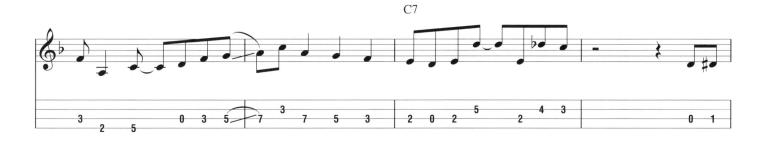

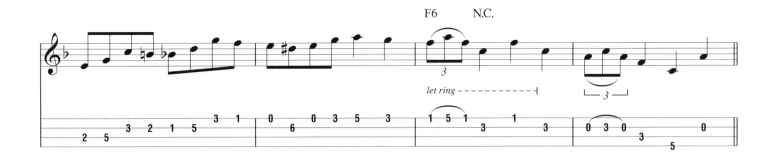

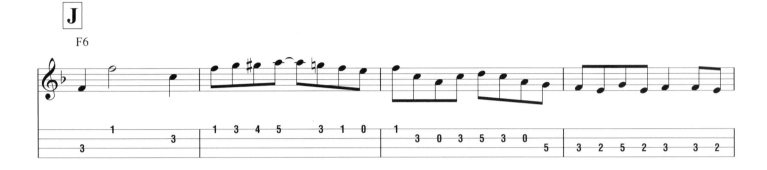

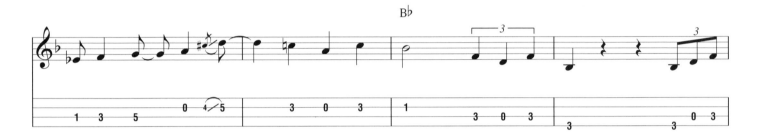

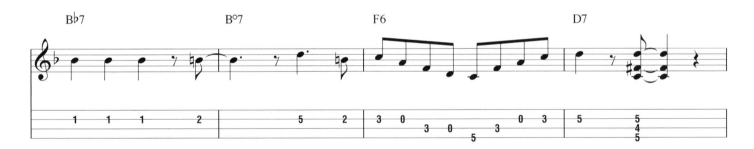

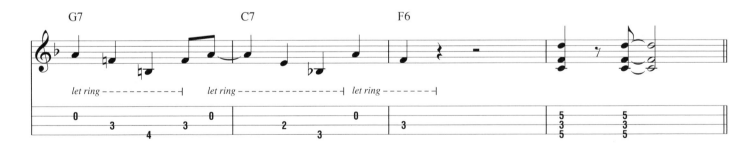

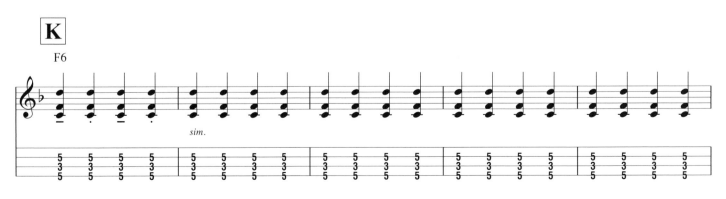

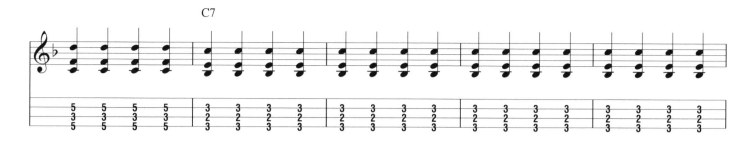

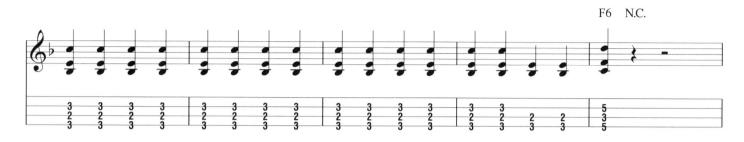

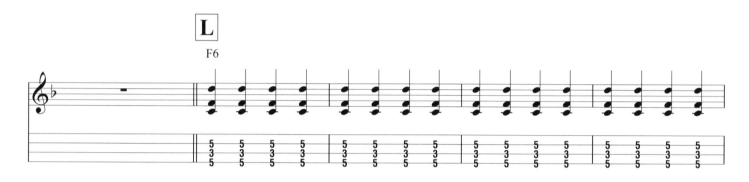

L

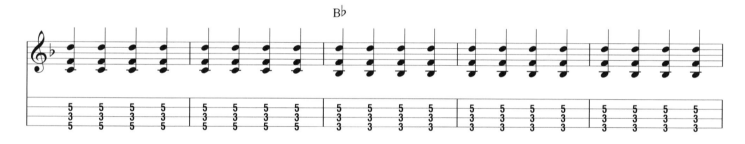

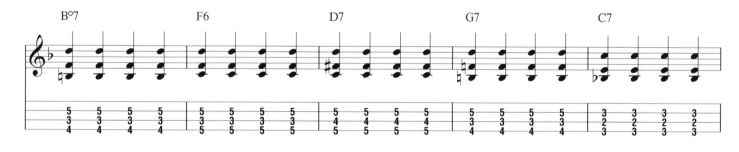

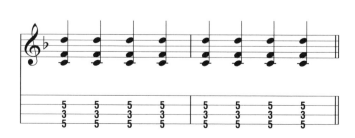

D.S. al Coda

 Coda

The Sheik of Araby

Words by Harry B. Smith and Francis Wheeler
Music by Ted Snyder

TRACK 13

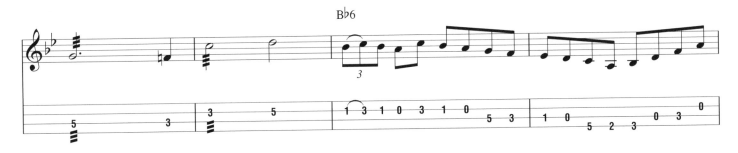

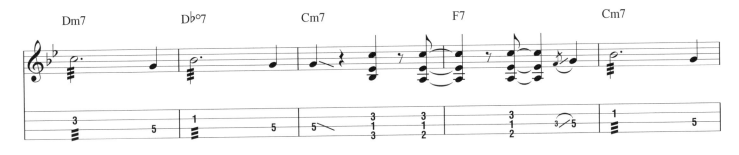

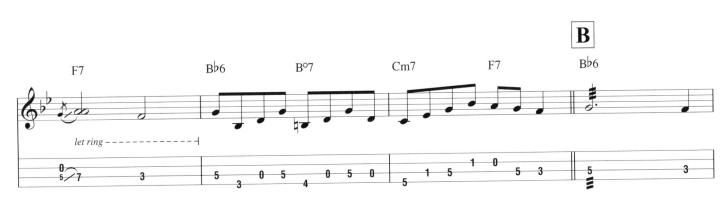

Copyright © 2015 by HAL LEONARD CORPORATION
International Copyright Secured   All Rights Reserved

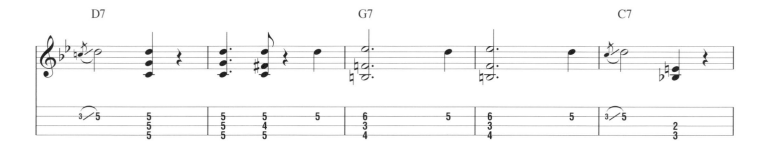

C

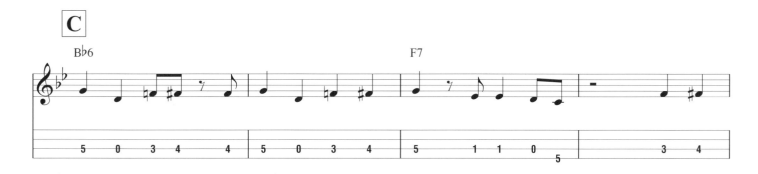

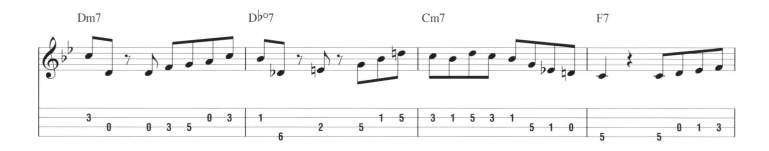

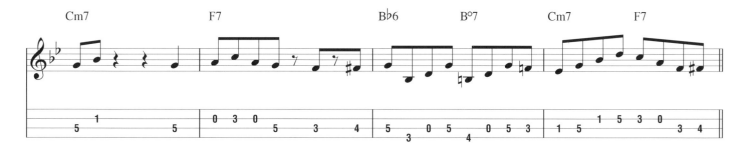

D

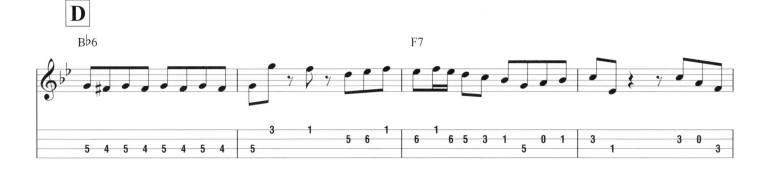

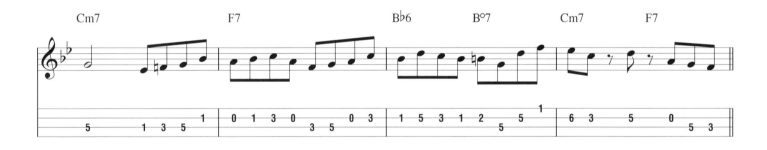

E

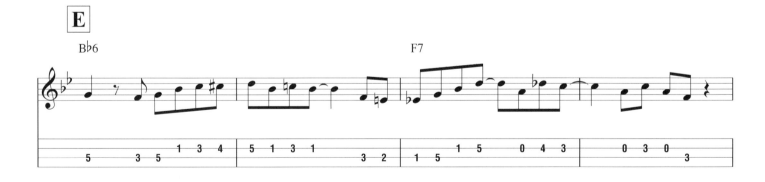

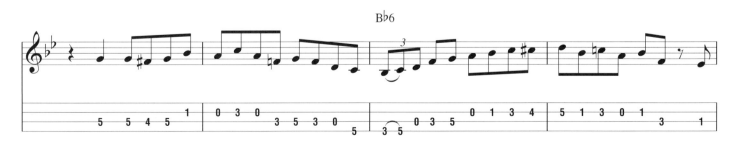

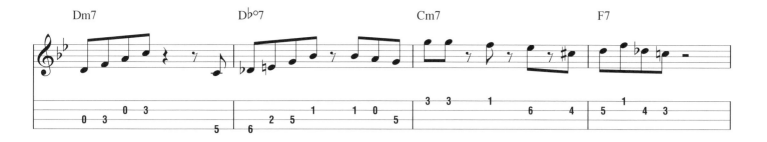

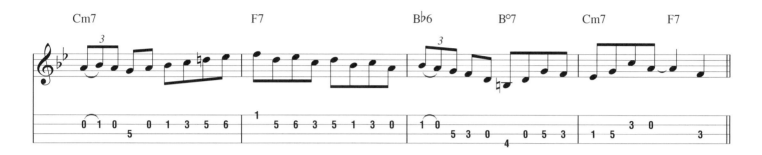

F

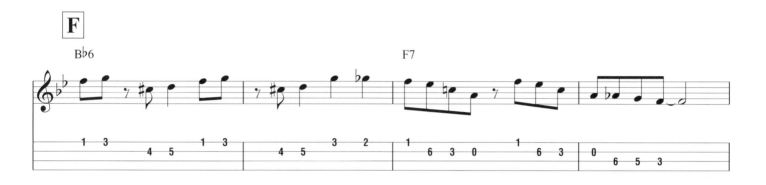

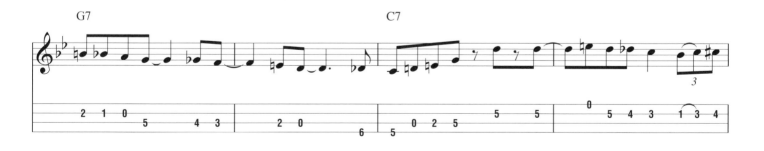

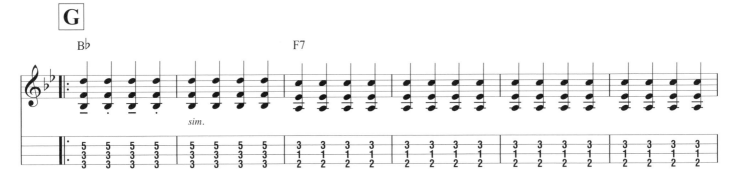

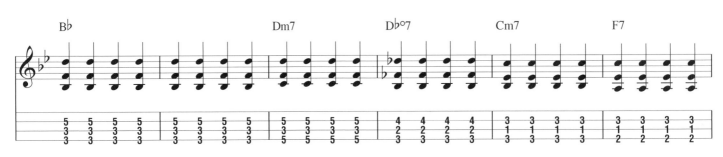

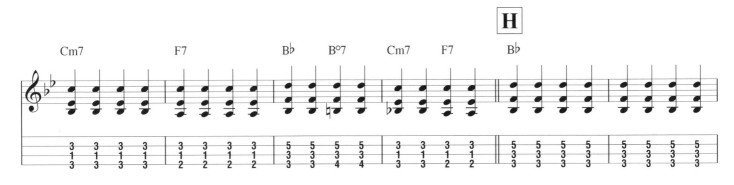

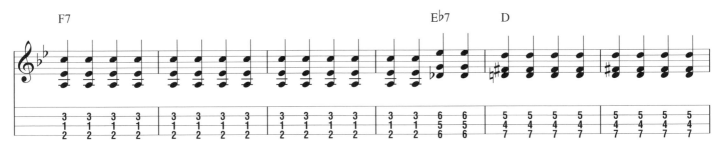

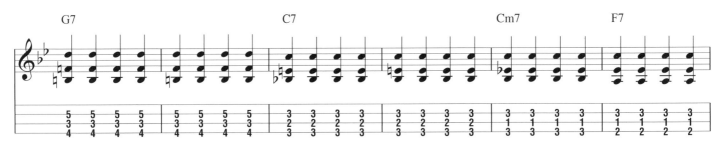

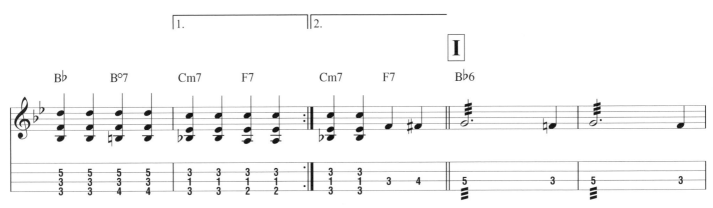

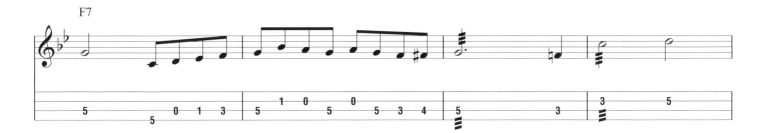

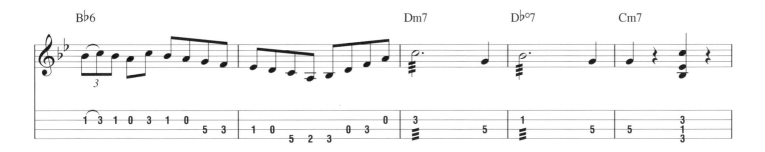

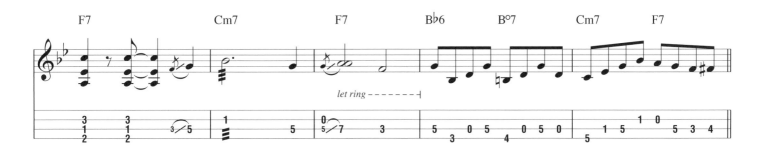

J

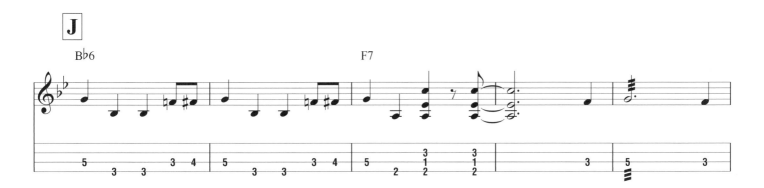

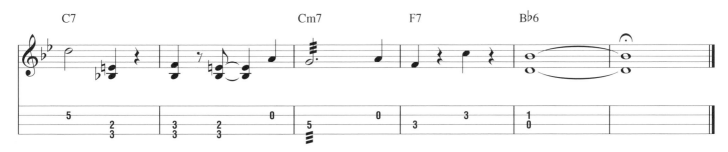

MANDOLIN NOTATION LEGEND

Mandolin music can be notated three different ways: on a *musical staff*, in *tablature*, and in *rhythm slashes*.

RHYTHM SLASHES are written above the staff. Strum chords in the rhythm indicated. Use the chord diagrams found at the top of the first page of the transcription for the appropriate chord voicings.

THE MUSICAL STAFF shows pitches and rhythms and is divided by bar lines into measures. Pitches are named after the first seven letters of the alphabet.

TABLATURE graphically represents the mandolin fretboard. Each of the four horizontal lines represents each of the four courses of strings, and each number represents a fret.

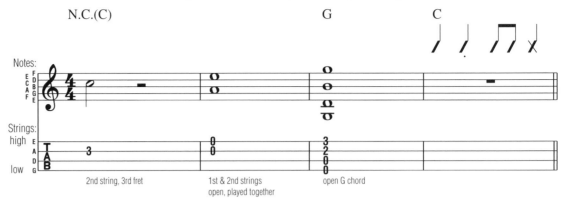

2nd string, 3rd fret | 1st & 2nd strings open, played together | open G chord

Definitions for Special Mandolin Notation

MUTED STRING(S): Lightly touch a string with the edge of your fret-hand finger while fretting a note on an adjacent string, causing the muted string to be unheard. Muting all of the strings with the fingers of the fret-hand while strumming the strings with the picking hand produces a percussive effect.

HAMMER-ON: Strike the first (lower) note with one finger, then sound the higher note (on the same string) with another finger by fretting it without picking.

PULL-OFF: Place both fingers on the notes to be sounded. Strike the first note and, without picking, pull the finger off to sound the second (lower) note.

LEGATO SLIDE: Strike the first note and then slide the same fret-hand finger up or down to the second note. The second note is not struck.

SHIFT SLIDE: Same as the legato slide except the second note is struck.

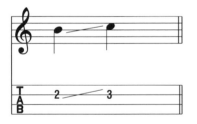

HALF-STEP BEND: Strike the note and bend up ½ step.

GRACE NOTE BEND: Strike the note and immediately bend up as indicated.

TREMOLO PICKING: The note is picked rapidly and continuously.

Additional Musical Definitions

p *(piano)* • Play quietly.

mp *(mezzo-piano)* • Play moderately quiet.

mf *(mezzo-forte)* • Play moderately loud.

f *(forte)* • Play loudly.

cont. rhy. sim. • Continue strumming in similar rhythm.

N.C. *(no chord)* • Don't strum until the next chord symbol. Chord symbols in parentheses reflect implied harmony.

D.S. al Coda • Go back to the sign (𝄋), then play until the measure marked *"To Coda"*, then skip to the section labeled *"Coda."*

D.S.S. al Coda 2 • Go back to the double sign (𝄋𝄋), then play until the measure marked *"To Coda 2"*, then skip to the section labeled *"Coda 2."*

D.S. al Fine • Go back to the sign (𝄋), then play until the label *"Fine."*

 *(staccato)* • Play the note or chord short.

 *(ritard)* • Gradually slow down.

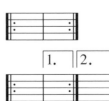 *(fermata)* • Hold the note or chord for an undetermined amount of time.

• Repeat measures between signs.

1. 2.
• When a repeated section has different endings, play the first ending only the first time and the second ending only the second time.

NOTE: Tablature numbers in parentheses mean:
1. The note is being sustained over a system (note in standard notation is tied), or
2. The note is sustained, but a new articulation (such as a hammer-on, pull-off or slide) begins.

Hal Leonard Mandolin Play-Along Series

The Mandolin Play-Along Series will help you play your favorite songs quickly and easily. Just follow the written music, listen to the CD to hear how the mandolin should sound, and then play along using the separate backing tracks. Standard notation and tablature are both included in the book. The CD is playable on any CD player, and is also enhanced so Mac and PC users can adjust the recording to any tempo without changing the pitch!

1. BLUEGRASS
Angeline the Baker • Billy in the Low Ground • Blackberry Blossom • Fisher's Hornpipe • Old Joe Clark • Salt Creek • Soldier's Joy • Whiskey Before Breakfast.
00702517 Book/CD Pack...$14.99

2. CELTIC
A Fig for a Kiss • The Kesh Jig • Morrison's Jig • The Red Haired Boy • Rights of Man • Star of Munster • The Star of the County Down • Temperence Reel.
00702518 Book/CD Pack...$14.99

3. POP HITS
Brown Eyed Girl • I Shot the Sheriff • In My Life • Mrs. Robinson • Stand by Me • Superstition • Tears in Heaven • You Can't Hurry Love.
00702519 Book/CD Pack...$14.99

4. J.S. BACH
Bourree in E Minor • Invention No.1 (Bach) • Invention No.2 (Bach) • Jesu, Joy of Man's Desiring • March in D Major • Minuet in G • Musette in D Major • Sleepers, Awake (Wachet Auf).
00702520 Book/CD Pack...$14.99

5. GYPSY SWING
After You've Gone • Avalon • China Boy • Dark Eyes • Indiana (Back Home Again in Indiana) • Limehouse Blues • The Sheik of Araby • Tiger Rag (Hold That Tiger).
00702521 Book/CD Pack...$14.99

6. ROCK HITS
Back in the High Life Again • Copperhead Road • Going to California • Ho Hey • Iris • Losing My Religion • Maggie May • Sunny Came Home.
00119367 Book/CD Pack...$16.99

7. ITALIAN CLASSICS
Come Back to Sorrento • La Spagnola • Mattinata • 'O Sole Mio • Oh Marie • Santa Lucia • Tarantella • Vieni Sul Mar.
00119368 Book/CD Pack...$16.99

8. MANDOLIN FAVORITES
Arrivederci Roma (Goodbye to Rome) • The Godfather (Love Theme) • Misirlou • Never on Sunday • Over the Rainbow • Spanish Eyes • That's Amoré (That's Love) • Theme from "Zorba the Greek".
00119494 Book/CD Pack...$16.99

9. CHRISTMAS CAROLS
Angels We Have Heard on High • Carol of the Bells • Go, Tell It on the Mountain • Hark! the Herald Angels Sing • Joy to the World • O Holy Night • Silent Night • We Wish You a Merry Christmas.
00119895 Book/CD Pack...$14.99

HAL•LEONARD® CORPORATION

7777 W. BLUEMOUND RD. P.O. BOX 13819 MILWAUKEE, WI 53213

Prices, contents, and availability subject to change without notice.

www.halleonard.com

Great Mandolin Publications

from

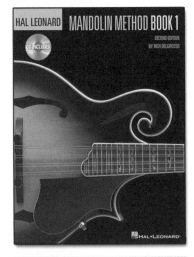
HAL LEONARD MANDOLIN METHOD BOOK 1

HAL LEONARD EASY SONGS FOR MANDOLIN MANDOLIN METHOD

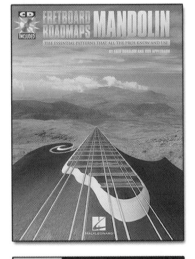
FRETBOARD ROADMAPS MANDOLIN

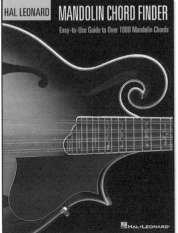
HAL LEONARD MANDOLIN CHORD FINDER

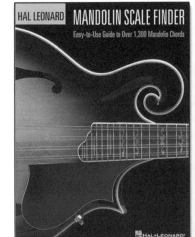
HAL LEONARD MANDOLIN SCALE FINDER

BILL MONROE 16 GEMS

O BROTHER, WHERE ART THOU?

THE ULTIMATE BLUEGRASS MANDOLIN CONSTRUCTION MANUAL

HAL LEONARD MANDOLIN METHOD *INCLUDES TAB*

Noted mandolinist and teacher Rich Del Grosso has authored this excellent mandolin method that features great playable tunes in several styles (bluegrass, country, folk, blues) in standard music notation and tablature. The optional audio features play-along duets.

00699296 Book Only $7.99
00695102 Book/CD Pack $15.99

EASY SONGS FOR MANDOLIN

SUPPLEMENTARY SONGBOOK TO THE HAL LEONARD MANDOLIN METHOD

20 songs to play as you learn mandolin: Annie's Song • California Dreamin' • Let It Be • Puff the Magic Dragon • Scarborough Fair • Where Have All the Flowers Gone? • and more.

00695865 Book Only $7.99
00695866 Book/CD Pack $15.99

FRETBOARD ROADMAPS – MANDOLIN *INCLUDES TAB*

THE ESSENTIAL PATTERNS THAT ALL THE PROS KNOW AND USE

by Fred Sokolow and Bob Applebaum

The latest installment in our popular Fretboard Roadmaps series is a unique book/CD pack for all mandolin players. The CD includes 48 demonstration tracks for the exercises that will teach players to: play all over the fretboard, in any key; increase their chord, scale and lick vocabulary; play chord-based licks, moveable major and blues scales, first-position major scales and double stops; and more! Includes easy-to-follow diagrams and instructions for all levels of players.

00695357 Book/CD Pack $12.95

MANDOLIN CHORD FINDER

EASY-TO-USE GUIDE TO OVER 1,000 MANDOLIN CHORDS

BY CHAD JOHNSON

Learn to play chords on the mandolin with this comprehensive, yet easy-to-use book. The Hal Leonard Mandolin Chord Finder contains over 1,000 chord diagrams for the most important 28 chord types, including three voicings for each chord. Also includes a lesson on chord construction, and a fingerboard chart of the mandolin neck!

00695739 9" X 12" Edition $6.95
00695740 6" X 9" Edition $5.99

MANDOLIN SCALE FINDER

EASY-TO-USE GUIDE TO OVER 1,300 MANDOLIN SCALES

by Chad Johnson

Presents scale diagrams for the most often-used scales and modes in an orderly and easily accessible fashion. Use this book as a reference guide or as the foundation for creating an in-depth practice routine. Includes multiple patterns for each scale, a lesson on scale construction, and a fingerboard chart of the mandolin neck.

00695779 9" X 12" Edition $6.95
00695782 6" X 9" Edition $5.95

BILL MONROE – 16 GEMS *INCLUDES TAB*

Authentic mandolin transcriptions of these classics by the Father of Bluegrass: Blue Grass Breakdown • Blue Grass Special • Can't You Hear Me Calling • Goodbye Old Pal • Heavy Traffic Ahead • I'm Going Back to Old Kentucky • It's Mighty Dark to Travel • Kentucky Waltz • Nobody Loves Me • Old Crossroad Is Waitin' • Remember the Cross • Shine Hallelujah Shine • Summertime Is Past and Gone • Sweetheart You Done Me Wrong • Travelin' This Lonesome Road • True Life Blues.

00690310 Mandolin Transcriptions $12.95

O BROTHER, WHERE ART THOU? *INCLUDES TAB*

Perfect for beginning to advanced players, this collection contains both note-for-note transcribed mandolin solos, as well as mandolin arrangements of the melody lines for 11 songs from this Grammy-winning Album of the Year: Angel Band • The Big Rock Candy Mountain • Down to the River to Pray • I Am a Man of Constant Sorrow • I Am Weary (Let Me Rest) • I'll Fly Away • In the Highways (I'll Be Somewhere Working for My Lord) • In the Jailhouse Now • Indian War Whoop • Keep on the Sunny Side • You Are My Sunshine. Chord diagrams provided for each song match the chords from the original recording, and all songs are in their original key. Includes tab, lyrics and a mandolin notation legend.

00695762... $12.99

THE ULTIMATE BLUEGRASS MANDOLIN CONSTRUCTION MANUAL

by Roger H. Siminoff

This is the most complete step-by-step treatise ever written on building an acoustical string instrument. Siminoff, a renowned author and luthier, applies over four decades of experience to guide beginners to pros through detailed chapters on wood selection, cutting, carving, shaping, assembly, inlays, fretting, binding and assembly of an F-style mandolin.

00331088... $34.95

Prices, contents and availability are subject to change without notice.

FOR MORE INFORMATION, SEE YOUR LOCAL MUSIC DEALER, OR WRITE TO:

HAL•LEONARD® CORPORATION

7777 W. BLUEMOUND RD. P.O. BOX 13819 MILWAUKEE, WI 53213

Visit Hal Leonard online at **www.halleonard.com**